Nuclear Power

by Tracy Vonder Brink

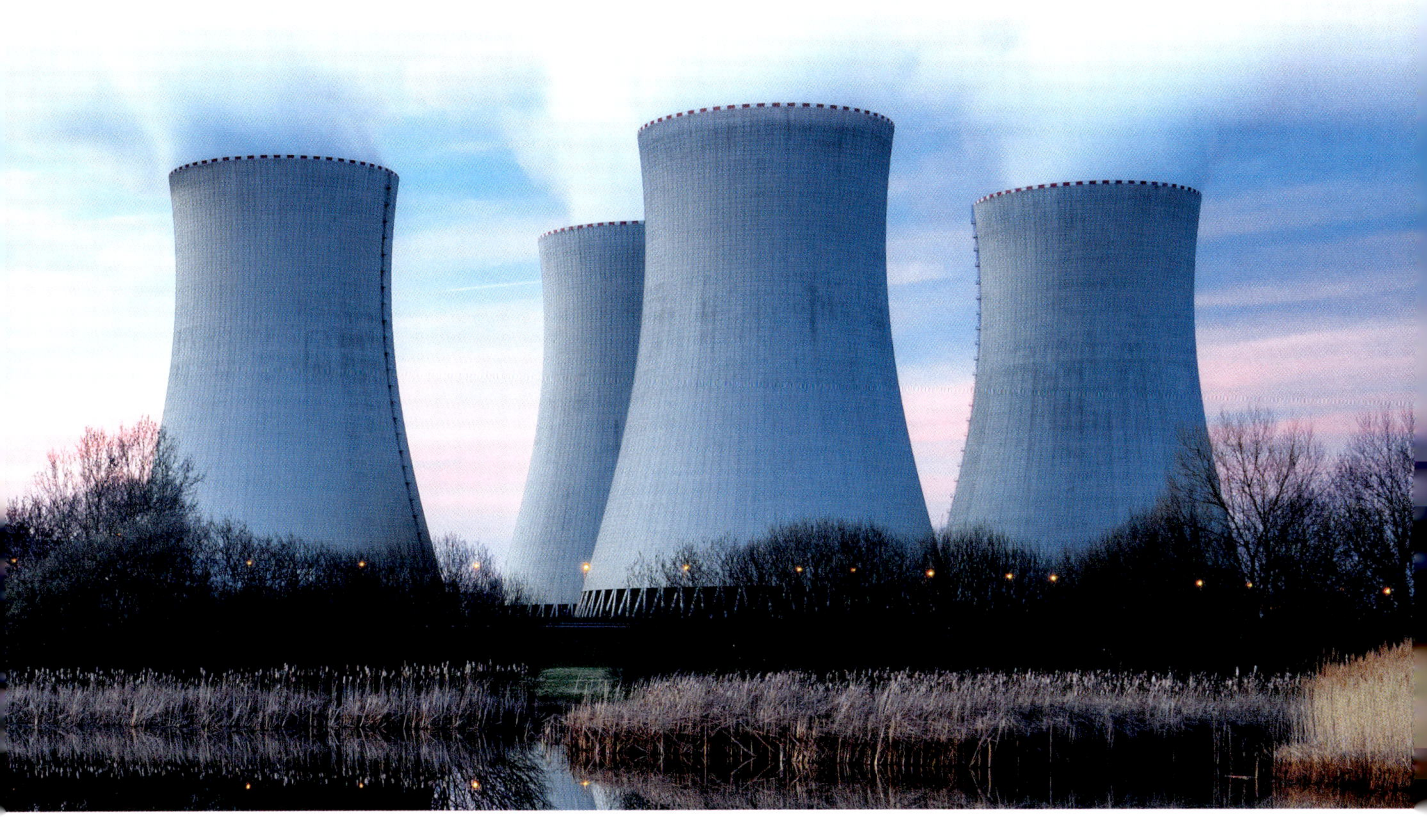

A Crabtree Crown Book

School-to-Home Support for Caregivers and Teachers

This appealing book is designed to teach students about core subject areas. Students will build upon what they already know about the subject, and engage in topics that they want to learn more about. Here are a few guiding questions to help readers build their comprehension skills. Possible answers appear here in red.

Before Reading:

What do I know about nuclear power?

- *I know nuclear energy is powerful.*
- *I know nuclear power plants are big.*

What do I want to learn about this topic?

- *I want to know how nuclear power makes electricity.*
- *I want to learn how scientists split atoms.*

During Reading:

I'm curious to know...

- *I'm curious to know how electricity created by nuclear power goes to a building.*
- *I'm curious to know how nuclear power plants work.*

How is this like something I already know?

- *I know buildings have electricity.*
- *I know nuclear power plants make power.*

After Reading:

What was the author trying to teach me?

- *The author was trying to teach me what nuclear power is.*
- *The author was trying to teach me how nuclear power can replace fossil fuels.*

How did the photographs and captions help me understand more?

- *The photographs helped me understand how nuclear power works.*
- *The captions gave me extra information.*

Table of Contents

Chapter 1: Energy and Fuel

We need energy for everything we do. Energy heats our homes. Our bodies use it to live. It fuels our cars. But what is energy?

In science, work is energy moving from one object to another. Your feet pushing against your bike's pedals are doing work that makes the bike move.

Energy is the ability to do work or to make something happen. Energy is everywhere. It comes in different forms. Heat, light, and sound are all forms of energy. The lights in your home use electrical energy.

Transforming Energy

Energy can be transformed, or changed, from one form to another. Energy changes forms when it is used to make something happen. Wood has energy locked inside it. Burning the wood changes its energy into heat and light.

Heat and light are two forms of energy.

A fuel is something that is changed in some way to produce energy. Wood is a fuel because burning it releases heat and light. Food is fuel for your body. Your body breaks down what you eat and uses it as energy.

Fossil Fuels

Fossil fuels are nonrenewable energy sources. Nonrenewable means they cannot be replaced.

We use fuels to make heat and power. Coal, oil, and natural gas are fuels. They are burned to release their energy. They all come from underneath the ground and they formed over millions of years. These types of fuels are called fossil fuels. If we use them up, they cannot be replaced.

Climate Change

Fossil fuels give off **carbon dioxide** when they are burned. Carbon dioxide collects in a layer around Earth. This layer traps heat and warms the planet. As Earth becomes warmer, its **climate** changes. We need energy sources that will not run out and that will not change the climate. We need **alternative** sources of energy. One such source is nuclear power.

Climate change harms people and animals. Impacts of climate change include higher temperatures and changes in rainfall. This can lead to wildfires and less water for crops. These changes affect where people and animals live and the food that they eat.

Chapter 2: Where Does Nuclear Power Come From?

You, your school, your best friend... everything around you that takes up space and has weight is matter. It is all made of atoms.

Matter and Atoms

Matter is anything that has weight and takes up space. Matter is made of tiny units called atoms. The nucleus is an atom's center.

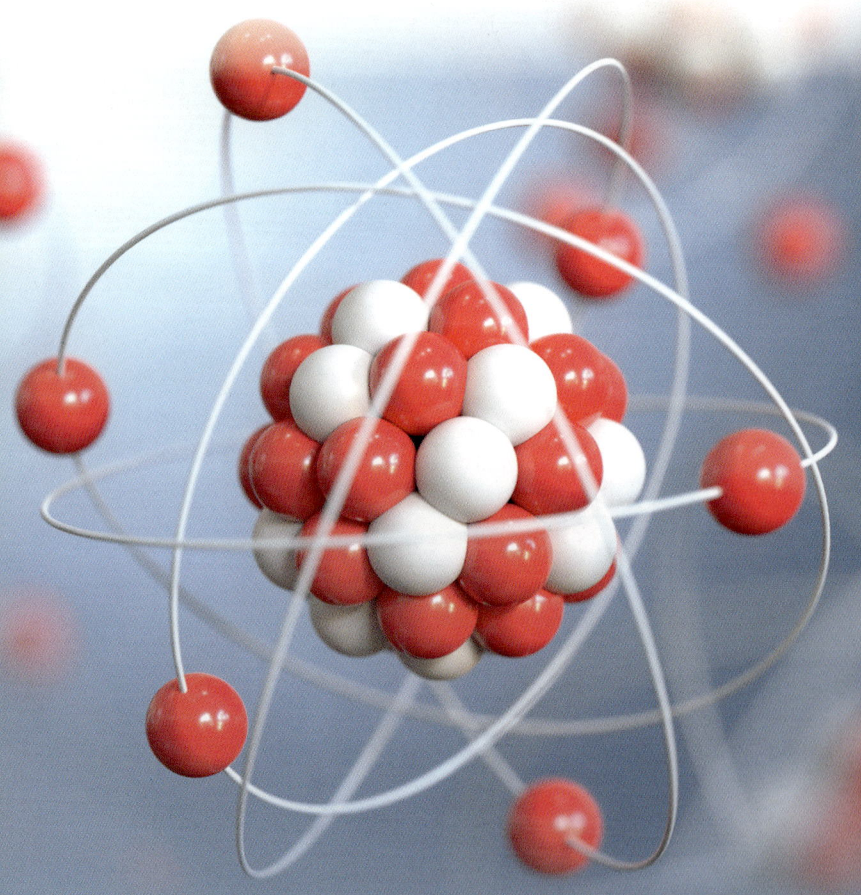

Atoms are too small to see without special tools.

An atom is tiny, but a lot of force holds it together. The nucleus consists of protons, that have a positive charge, and neutrons, that have no charge. Electrons surround the nucleus. They have a negative charge.

Splitting Atoms

Splitting an atom releases its energy. Scientists split an atom by using a special machine to fire neutrons at it. The extra neutrons make the atom break.

Crushing rocks that hold uranium helps separate it for use.

Uranium is found in some rocks. Kazakhstan produces the most uranium in the world.

Splitting atoms in this way is called fission. Scientists used fission to split an atom for the first time in 1932. In 1938, they discovered that uranium gave off more energy than other **elements** when split.

Chain Reactions

An atom split by fission throws off more neutrons. If the neutrons hit a nearby atom, it may also split. Then that atom throws off neutrons, and so on. Atoms causing other atoms to split is called a chain reaction.

A neutron fired at an atom's nucleus splits the nucleus into smaller parts.

Splitting one uranium atom can set off a chain reaction. The chain reaction happens quickly and gives off even more energy than one atom alone. The energy is released as heat.

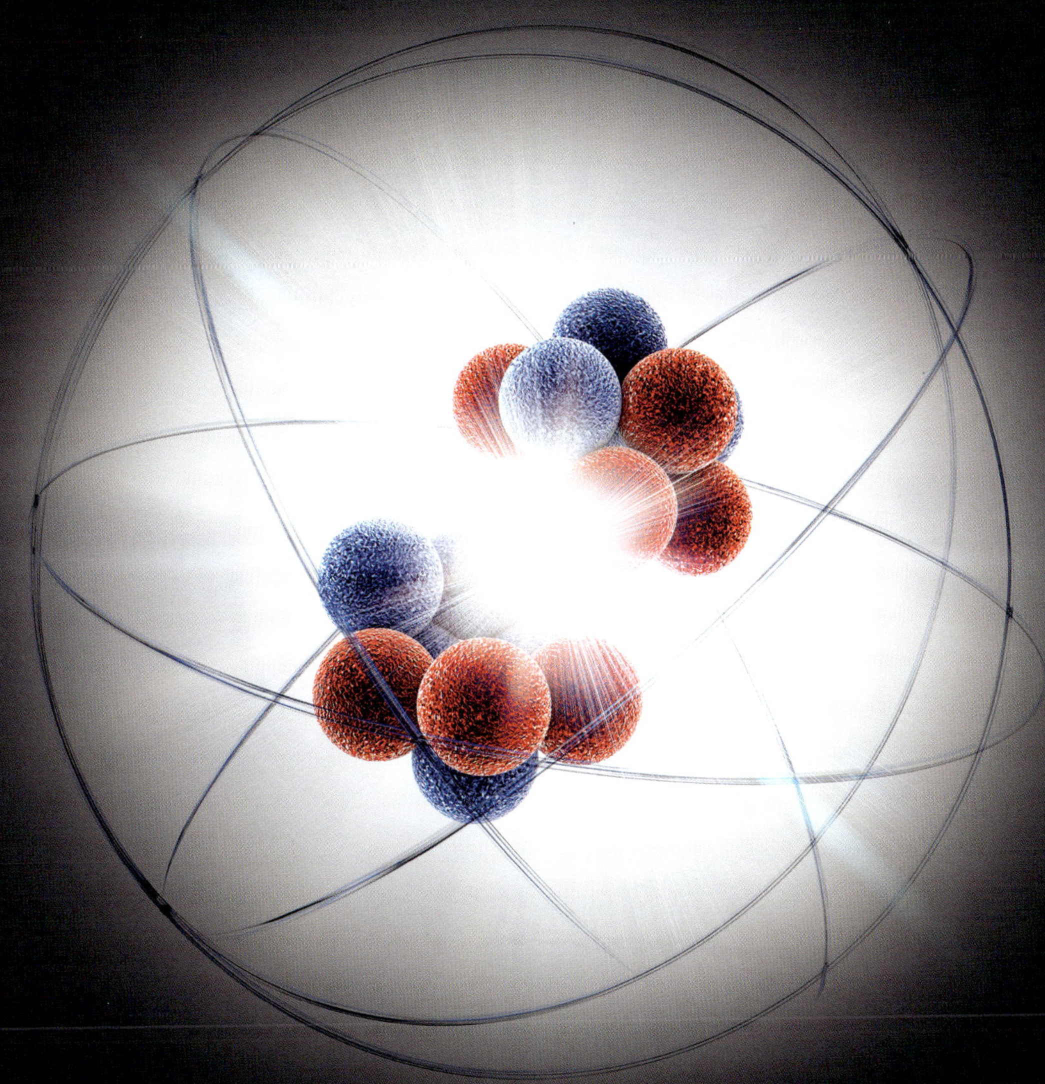

All nuclear power plants use nuclear fission.

Chapter 3: Creating Nuclear Power

About 400 fuel pellets fit in one rod. Half of one pellet can make enough electricity to power a home for six months.

Uranium can be turned into fuel pellets for a nuclear **power plant**. The pellets go into metal tubes, called fuel rods. A large power plant might have 51,000 rods and more than 18 million pellets.

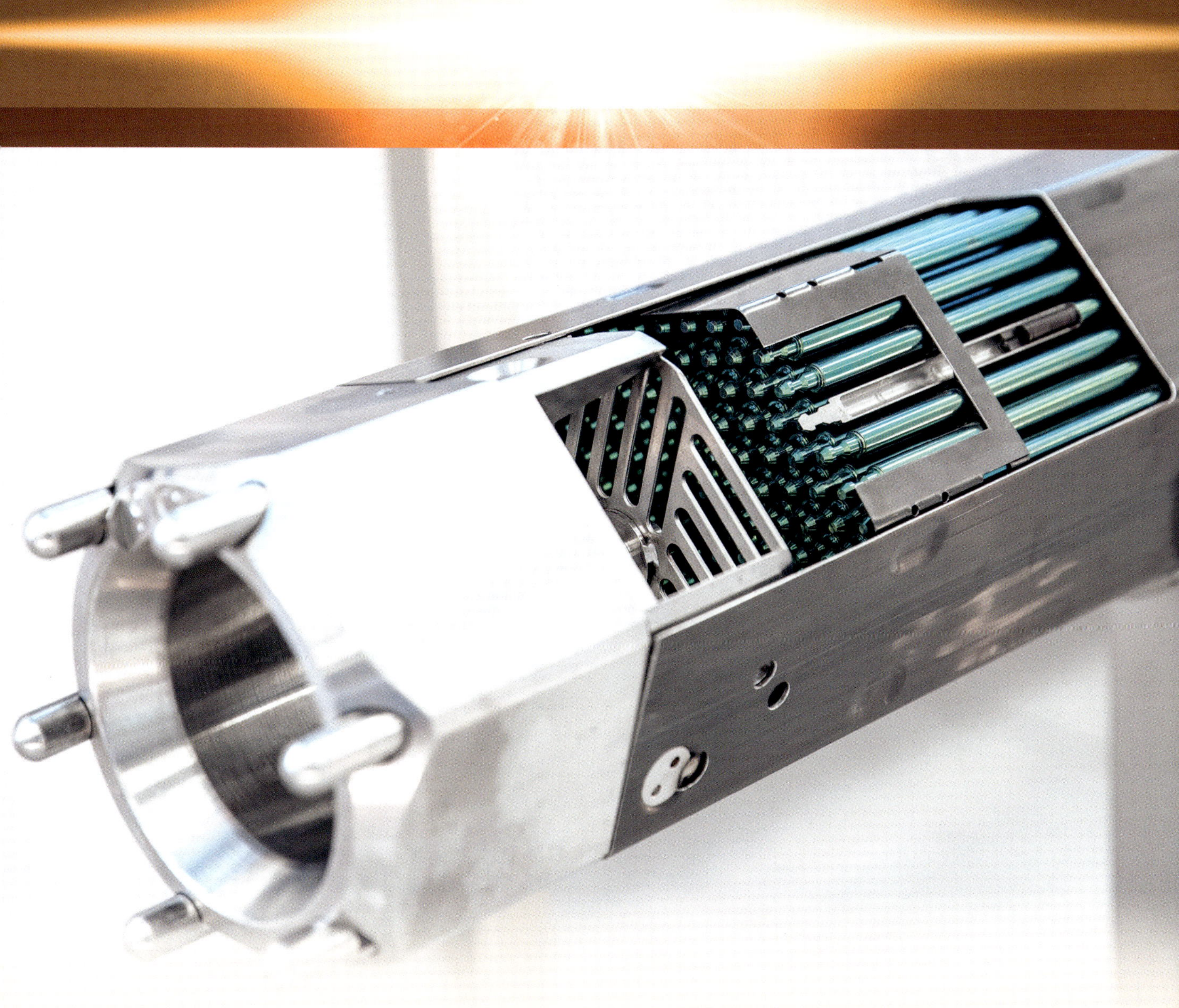

A nuclear power plant also has startup rods and control rods. All the rods are placed together inside a **reactor**. When the control rods are lifted away from the startup rods, neutrons from the startup rods hit the uranium fuel pellets. The atoms split and release energy. To stop fission, control rods are lowered to block the startup rods' neutrons.

Using Nuclear Power

How does heat from splitting atoms create electricity? Heat boils water inside the nuclear power plant like a giant teakettle. Boiling water releases steam. The steam pushes against blades connected to a generator. The blades turn, and the generator makes electricity.

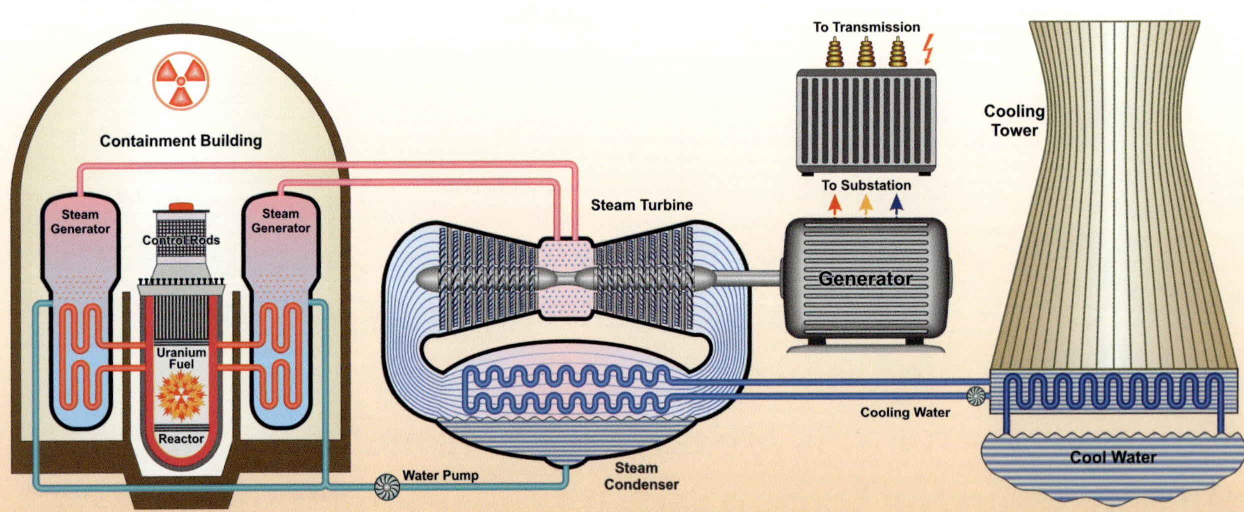

Some cooling towers turn steam back into water so it can be returned to the power plant and used again.

Chapter 4: Powering a City

Electricity in a power grid may come from both nonrenewable and alternative energy sources.

The electricity generated by nuclear power plants travels through power lines to a **substation**. The substation changes the electricity into a form that can be sent to a **power grid**. All sources of electricity feed into the same power grids.

Smaller substations carry the electricity to towns and cities. Power lines above or below the ground connect them. Electricity flows from the substation into homes, businesses, streetlights, and more.

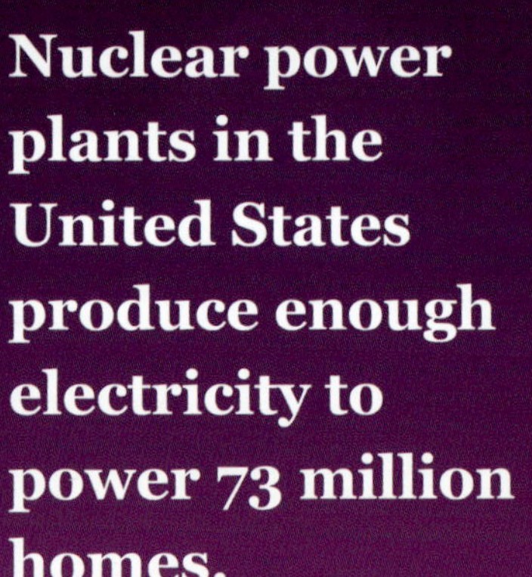

Nuclear power plants in the United States produce enough electricity to power 73 million homes.

Chapter 5: Challenges of Nuclear Power

When the uranium in fuel rods is used up, the rods must be removed. The old rods give off **radioactive** energy and are harmful to people and animals. Old rods must be stored safely. It may take thousands of years before the waste is no longer harmful.

Used fuel rods are sometimes stored in special steel containers.

Cost to Build

The U.S. state of South Carolina planned to build two new nuclear reactors. The cost was too much, and the project was stopped.

Nuclear power plants are very expensive to build. In the United States, a new nuclear power plant in Georgia cost more than 27 billion dollars. Nuclear power plants may take around 10 years to build.

Limited Uranium

Uranium is made into a form called yellowcake before becoming fuel for a nuclear power plant.

Like fossil fuels, uranium cannot be replaced once it is used up. It is thought that the world's uranium supply will last around 80 years. After that, there will be none to power nuclear plants.

Nuclear Accidents

There have been few serious nuclear accidents, but people worry there could be more. In 1986, an accident at the Chernobyl nuclear power plant in Ukraine killed 31 people and harmed thousands more. More than 300,000 people had to leave their homes in the area and were never able to return. Even today, the area around Chernobyl remains closed.

In 2011, an earthquake near Japan's Fukushima Daiichi power plant knocked out its systems. Three reactors overheated, and 10,000 people had to leave their homes. Fukushima Daiichi is still closed today.

Chapter 6: Possible Nuclear Power

Twelve small reactors could power about 540,000 homes. The United States, Russia, China, and Canada all plan to build small reactors.

Mini nuclear reactors are starting to be built around the world because they are smaller and simpler to build. The smaller reactors are about one-third of the size of a regular nuclear reactor. They also cost less and are faster to build, and they may be safer.

Fusion

Fusion releases energy from atoms by smashing them together. Fusion is what powers the Sun. It does not need uranium to work. It would produce less waste. But scientists have not yet figured out how to build a fusion power plant.

Chapter 7: The Future of Nuclear Power

Nuclear power produces no carbon dioxide. A nuclear power plant can be relied on to make electricity 24 hours a day, seven days a week. Small nuclear energy sources also power spacecraft and some submarines.

Building nuclear power plants has slowed in favor of other alternative energy sources, but about 50 new nuclear power plants are planned around the world. Today, nuclear power produces about 10 percent of the world's electricity. Will it provide more in the future?

Glossary

alternative (ahl-TUR-nuh-tive): Something that may be chosen instead of something else

carbon dioxide (CAR-bun dye-OX-ide): A gas that is produced when people or animals breathe out or when certain fuels are burned

climate (KLEYE-muht): The usual weather conditions of a particular place

element (EH-luh-muhnt): A pure substance made from a single type of atom

power grid (PAU-ur GRID): A connected system for delivering electrical power from power plants to homes and businesses

power plant (PAU-ur PLANT): A place where electricity is made

radioactive (ray-dee-oh-ACK-tive): Having a dangerous form of energy

reactor (ree-ACK-tr): The central part of a nuclear power plant where fission takes place

substation (SUHB-stay-shn): Equipment that makes electricity usable for people

Index

Comprehension Questions

1. What powers a nuclear power plant?
   a. Burning uranium atoms
   b. Splitting uranium atoms
   c. Smashing uranium atoms together
2. How is fission in a nuclear reactor started?
   a. Control rods are lifted away
   b. Control rods are lowered
   c. Startup rods spin around
3. What is one of the challenges of nuclear power?
   a. Nuclear power uses a lot of land
   b. Fission is slow
   c. Uranium will run out
4. True or False: Nonrenewable energy sources can be replaced.
5. True or False: Splitting uranium atoms can cause a chain reaction.

Comprehension questions answer key: 1. b 2. a 3. c 4. False 5. True

About the Author

Tracy Vonder Brink loves true stories and facts. She has written more than 20 books for kids and is a contributing editor for three children's science magazines. Tracy lives in Cincinnati, Ohio, with her husband, two daughters, and two rescue dogs.

Written by: Tracy Vonder Brink
Designed by: Jennifer Bowers
Series Development: James Earley
Proofreader: Melissa Boyce
Educational Consultant: Marie Lemke M.Ed.
Print Coordinator: Katherine Berti

Photographs: cover ©2017 vlastas/Shutterstock, ©R2D2/Shutterstock; p.4 ©2021 Lin Xiu Xiu/Shutterstock; p.5 ©2015 Africa Studio/Shutterstock; p.6 ©2020 Natalia Leinonen/Shutterstock; p.7 ©2016 Tatjana Baibakova/Shutterstock; p8. ©2020 Sunshine Seeds/Shutterstock; p.9 ©2009 Mark Smith/Shutterstock; p.10 ©2019 koya979/Shutterstock; p.11 ©2016 Andrea Danti/Shutterstock; p.12 ©2012 Fineart1/Shutterstock; p.13 ©2021 RHJPhtotoandilustration/Shutterstock; p.14 ©Peter Hermes Furian/Shutterstock; p.15 ©2013 jules2000/Shutterstock; p.16 ©2018 Peter Sobolev/Shutterstock; p.17 ©2019 Parilov/Shutterstock; p.18 ©Fouad A. Saad/Shutterstock; p.19 ©2017 Jenson/Shutterstock; p.20 ©2021 yelantsevv/Shutterstock; p.21 ©2019 Krysja/Shutterstock; p.22 ©2021 Alien Cat/Shutterstock; p.23 ©2008 Kristina Postnikova/Shutterstock; p.24 ©2019 lux3000/Shutterstock; p.25 ©2019 Santiherllor/Shutterstock; p.26 ©2021 Marko Aliaksandr/Shutterstock; p.27 ©2019 Quardia/Shutterstock; p.28-29 ©2018 J. Quendag/Shutterstock

Library and Archives Canada Cataloguing in Publication

Available at the Library and Archives Canada

Library of Congress Cataloging-in-Publication Data

Available at the Library of Congress

Crabtree Publishing Company

www.crabtreebooks.com 1-800-387-7650

Published in the United States
Crabtree Publishing
347 Fifth Avenue
Suite 1402-145
New York, NY, 10016

Published in Canada
Crabtree Publishing
616 Welland Ave.
St. Catharines, ON
L2M 5V6

Printed in the U.S.A./072022/CG20220201